Calming the Waters

A Parent's Guide to Autism Spectrum Disorder

To my boy, my love:

"I hope when you count the stars you begin with yourself, and may you embrace the moonlight with your dreams."

-Dodinsky

INTRODUCTION — 6

CHAPTER ONE — 10

What is Autism? — 10
Causes of Autism Spectrum Disorder — 11
Different Types of Autism Spectrum Disorder — 12
Autism Spectrum Disorder — 12

Rett Syndrom — 13
Pervasive Developmental Disorder-Not Otherwise Specified (PDD-NOS)AA
How is Autism Spectrum Disorder diagnosed? — 13
Symptoms of Autism Spectrum Disorder — 14
Behaviors — 15
Theories About The Cause of Autism — 20

CHAPTER TWO — 22

Effects on education and academic performance in children with ASD — 22
Main Types of Disability Support for Students with ASD in Public — 25
A Brief History of Special Education Laws in North America — 28

CHAPTER THREE — 30

Tips on Parenting Children with ASD — 31
Developing Sensory Processing Skills to Cope with ASD — 32
Developing Motor Skills to Cope with ASD — 35
Creating an Individualized Communication Plan for ASD Children — 36
Other Communication Skills that Can Help Alleviate Behavioral Issues. — 38

CHAPTER FOUR — 42

SCHOOL AND LEARNING- GETTING THE RIGHT EDUCATION FOR A CHILD   42
HOW TO COPE WITH BEHAVIORS FOR THE CHILD IN THE SCHOOL   52

CHAPTER FIVE   56

THE TRANSITION TO ADULTHOOD   56
Finding a support group   57
Having a spouse or partner   58
Letting your child make choices   60
Creating a social support group   63

CHAPTER SIX   64

HELPING A CHILD WITH ASD   64
EARLY INTERVENTION AND THERAPIES   66
Practitioner Services: 66
THERAPIES: 67
Occupational Therapy: 68
Speech Therapy: 70
Psychological therapy: 72
Behavioral therapy: 73
HOW PARENTS CAN HELP CHILDREN WITH ASD   76

CHAPTER SEVEN   78

HELPFUL TIPS FOR PARENTS OF AUTISTIC CHILDREN IN POVERTY   78
FINANCIAL ASSISTANCE PROGRAMS FOR CHILDREN WITH AUTISM IN POVERTY   80

CONCLUSION   83

ACKNOLEDGEMENTS   85

REFERENCES	**86**
QUOTES	**88**
ABOUT THE AUTHOR	**89**

Introduction

"Your child has autism" is not what any parent wants to hear. Yet here I was at the doctor's office hearing those words like they were spoken in a foreign language.

What did that mean for my boy and us as a family?

15 years later, as I am writing this book, I know what it meant for our family and wished that there would have been more resources and information out there at the time. I hope my book will be just that. It should give an insight to what's laying ahead and hope for you and your family.

How did you feel when you first heard your child had autism spectrum disorder? It might have been an absolute bombshell, with no warning and time to prepare. As a parent, many questions can be answered, some making you feel very uncomfortable. But once the initial shock has subsided and you've got a better understanding of what needs to be done, it can be quite manageable.

In this guide we'll help parents of children with autism spectrum disorder get started on their journey towards dealing with their child's condition. Kids in North America are more likely to receive services for ASD related issues through early intervention programs. This is a very important step that needs to be taken early and many can participate from the time their child is identified and on the way to get diagnosed.

This guide will cover what it takes to get your child into these programs and on the road to success.

Parents can best help their child with autism spectrum disorder by learning as much as possible about them. There are many different types of autism spectrum disorders; each comes with its own challenges. The diagnose itself does not define your child's personality or the unique needs he has. Every child on the spectrum is different, although some of the behaviours might be similar. Usually sensory issues are very pronounced and each child will have to have their own "sensory diet". If sensitive to noise ear muffs, head phones with calming music or ear plugs are helpful. Sensitivity to light is less often the case but here also a baseball hat or sun glasses have a calming effect.

Knowledge is power when it comes to dealing with autism spectrum disorder. As a parent, you know this first hand and help your child navigate the world in a way that feels comfortable. The world at large is becoming more open minded about children with different types of disabilities than ever before.

N.B: This guide is provided by the Author, a parent of an autistic child who is also an Educational Assistant with over 10 years of experience now willing to share her knowledge with you in this book.

This book aims to assist parents and educators alike in understanding how autism affects a child's social and cognitive development as it relates to education and how to help them. The book discusses common misconceptions about autism, symptoms of ASD and resources for dealing with ASD for both the adult with ASD and their family members. Also included is some information on how to help with raising a child with autism and tips from experts on coping.

I hope this book is calming the waters a little for you…

One year into my son's diagnose, I found myself discouraged, tired and exhausted. I felt like a failure and it seemed despite all my efforts I just couldn't get through to him. I felt disconnected and I was afraid that I was letting down the person I loved most in this world, my little boy.

One night, lying awake in my bed, I had a vision. I saw myself sitting in a boat alone and my son was in a boat next to me. I was desperately trying to pull him into my boat but he just wouldn't budge…

Exhausted I surrendered and climbed into his boat. I sat behind him and let him be the captain, always ensuring he was safe navigating his own boat.

When I decided to let go of my idea of how he should be and let him be who he was, I became calm - and so did he. That was the day our true journey began and what a beautiful one it has been.

Chapter One

What is Autism?

"Autism" refers to a spectrum of disorders characterized by difficulties in social interaction, verbal and nonverbal communication and repetitive behavior. It manifests as a disorder that hinders one's ability to communicate and relate to others. Autism presents itself early in childhood.

Individuals with this disorder can have normal language skills and ordinary intelligence but experience problems in social interaction due to their specific way of behaviors. These challenges have been associated with differences in brain development. Although this disorder can be mild or severe, it affects each person differently.

Autism Spectrum Disorder is one of five pervasive developmental disorders that affect one child per 88, according to the statistics from the CDC (Centers for Disease Control and Prevention) - the research arm of the US Department of Health.

One effect autism spectrum disorder has on people's lives is that it often leads to difficulties in daily living skills such as self-care, social interactions, speech and working collaboratively in groups, making carrying out different tasks very difficult for the individual. Autism spectrum disorder also has a major impact on the child's parents, families, and relationships they have with other people. However, many treatment options can improve the quality of life.

Causes of Autism Spectrum Disorder

The exact cause of autism spectrum disorder is unknown, and research is still being carried out to determine its cause; some research points towards hereditary factors that might play a role others found environmental factors to be the cause. None of it has been proven at this point and we are still searching for the answers in solving the autism puzzle.

Autism is not caused by anything specific, and it cannot be prevented.

To aid parents who are looking for answers, we've compiled some of the most common causes that we came across:

Genetics: Some children are born with autism, and it's not always because of external reasons, like other health issues or vaccines. The same could be said about Schizophrenia, often found in families with a history of autism

Food intolerance: It is common for children to react to certain foods or medications. According to doctors, children who are sensitive to different foods are ten times more likely to have autism.

The Main Types of Autism Spectrum Disorder

There are 3 main types of autism:

Autism Spectrum Disorder, Rett Syndrome, Pervasive Developmental Disorder Not Otherwise Specified. The different types of autism all have different causes and treatments. In addition, each type of autism has its own unique characteristics.

Autism Spectrum Disorder

People with ASD often have difficulties in the following areas: social interactions connecting with others or seeking friendships. In the past it was said that a lack of emotions is part of the disorder but I believe quite the contrary is the case. Often feelings are on such a deep level that it is easier to block the feelings out. Specific hand gestures, noises and sometimes extreme reactions to changes in their daily routine. The former called Asperger's Syndrome is now under the umbrella of ASD. Being indifferent and eccentric is often a trademark as well as being extremely intelligent. Often there is a preoccupation with certain topics such as astronomy, dinosaurs etc.

Rett Syndrome

Rett syndrome is a genetic neurological disorder who affects more females than males. It is caused by a mutation on the X chromosome in the brain. It causes reduced head growth in babies, problems with speech and motor skills, social interaction and cognitive abilities.

Pervasive Developmental Disorder-Not Otherwise Specified (PDD-NOS)

People portray difficulties engaging in social interaction and communication and engage in repetitive movements. Often have difficulties adapting to changes in routine or environment.

How is Autism Spectrum Disorder diagnosed?

The diagnosis of autism spectrum disorder is based on the presenting symptoms, age at onset and family history. The diagnosis is made by combining the information obtained from the parents and medical personnel. The diagnosis is also confirmed by the fact that there is a difference in functioning between them and other people their age.

Some of the symptoms are avoiding eye contact, delayed speech and communication skills, reliance on rules and routines, being upset by relatively minor changes, unexpected reactions to sounds, tastes, sights, touch and smells, difficulties understanding other people's emotions.

The physician or psychologist will carry out tests that reveal certain patterns, which, combined with the above factors, will confirm a diagnosis of autism spectrum disorder. These tests include interviews, observation of social interactions, physical and neurological examination, developmental milestones assessment, and psychological testing such as IQ exams. One major test to detect autism spectrum disorder is the Autism Diagnostic Observation Schedule (ADOS).

Symptoms of Autism Spectrum Disorder

Autism spectrum disorder can be diagnosed as early as 18 months and is often detected when a child starts to show behavior issues. The symptoms vary greatly from person to person. The severity of the symptoms depends on the extent of brain involvement. Some children with autism spectrum disorder are very high functioning, meaning they may have an age level or higher intellectual ability and normal language development but still struggle with social interaction skills and challenges with verbal and nonverbal communication skills. There are many possible symptoms of autism spectrum disorder, and as the symptoms vary so greatly, they are a very varied group of challenges that affect each individual.

Some common symptoms include unusual body movements, two-tone speech, poor eye contact and a general absence of facial expressions. However, as the disorder is more likely to affect individuals with milder symptoms, they will often not have any insight into the underlying cause of their difficulties. Therefore, it can be difficult for parents of children with ASD to know what type of help may be suitable.

Another symptom that often affects individuals on the spectrum is repetitive behaviors, such as head banging and flapping. These are called stereotypic behaviors, and they can also result in injuries. Some people have a need to gather objects and items to gain comfort or reassurance. A phrase heard on TV or a movie might be repetitively recited.

Behaviors

Every behavior stems from an unfulfilled basic need. Dr. Glasser explains with what he calls **"Choice Theory Basic Needs"**. According to Dr. Glasser, all behavior is purposeful. It's our best attempt at the time, given our best knowledge and skills, to meet one or more of our basic human needs, which evolved over time and have become part of our genetic structure. These needs are the general motivation for everything we do.

1. **Surviva**l- This need is physical and includes the need for food, shelter and safety

2. **Love and Belonging** – This need is psychological and includes the need for relationships, friendship, giving and receiving affection, and feeling part of a group.

3. **Power**- to achieve and be competent, skilled, recognized, listened to and self-worth.

4. **Freedom**- The need for independence, autonomy, and choices.

5. **Fun**- pleasure, play, laugh.

A nonverbal boy on the spectrum and his mother loved to ride the bus together. They were waiting at the bus stop, and the boy was excited to ride the bus. The bus arrives, the doors open and he has a meltdown. The mother told me that happened every time, and she couldn't figure out what it was that she was missing. She noticed that he showed the same behavior when they went to the grocery store with automatic doors. She just didn't know what it was about automatic doors that upset him.

The next time they went to get the bus, she asked the bus driver if he would mind showing her son how the doors open and close on the bus. Luckily the bus driver was very accommodating and let the boy press the buttons for the doors so he could understand how they worked.

The mother knew there was something she was missing, and she figured it out. He was upset that he couldn't understand why those doors seemingly opened without anybody operating them, like a car or a house door that needed a physical approach. She also had the grocery store manager show her son the door shutter and opener. Problem solved, way to go, Mom!

Another young boy was getting upset every time he noticed the gas was getting lower on the gas display on his Dad's dashboard. He was concerned that they would run out of gas if the needle moved only slightly. Mom and Dad repeatedly explained that they had enough gas for days to go, but it continued to upset him and caused tantrums. In this case, a piece of cardboard covering up the gas display did the trick. Sometimes, keeping it simple is the key!

The following is the list of common autistic behaviors:

-They tend to withdraw in social situations, not wanting to be touched or hugged.

They won't want to share their toys and may not want anyone else using them. They might seem unapproachable or 'selfish.' This is because they don't want to share their world experiences and have trouble connecting socially. Autistic children may also seem detached from bodily sensations, like when they fall and don't react much. They are much more sensitive than their outward behavior might suggest.

They may crave sensory stimuli and have a very keen eye for detail.

- repetitiveness of certain actions, like rocking back and forth, flapping their hands, or lining up toys or other objects the same way every time. This behavior is referred to as 'stimming'. Stimming serves a few purposes for those who engage in it: it provides comfort, calms anxiety and soothes distress. Unfortunately, however, stimming can become too repetitive and the child might have a hard time to break out of it. In that case a distraction with a preferred object or activity can help.

- may not seem to be able to make friends easily. They may also display a stubborn attitude towards their needs and wants, which can often be misinterpreted as selfishness. They might easily feel overwhelmed in social situations and may just leave when they want to escape it or may just not be able to participate in the social activity that everyone else seems so interested in.

Parents and educators can use the following tips to cope with behaviors related to autism spectrum disorder:

-Communicate with your child using their verbal means of communication, e.g., an iPad or a keyboard with picture commands that you show them how to type on it if they can't speak verbally; this will ensure that you understand what your child wants or needs from you to feel safe or happy.

-Learn your child's 'favourite' messages and activities. It will be much easier to understand your family member when you know the signals they like to use. For example, if they smile when they love you or cry when they want a hug or a special toy. If your child is not physically affectionate, it is good to practice by giving them a massage or high five to learn how it feels on the inside. In my case my husband and I waited until our son was fast asleep and then held him as he didn't want physical touch when he was awake. I believe that all children have to feel a mother's and fathers touch to develop their sense of physical closeness. And let's be honest here: I am his Mom! I really needed and cherished my nightly snuggles with him. Today he is much more affectionate and able to give us hugs.

-Keep practicing behaviors that will move them in the right direction. Try to talk with your child as much as possible through sign language and text. The more you practice, the more you will learn about their feelings and what they want or don't want. Their frustration level will go down immensely once they figure out how to communicate

-Ask your child what they need or want even if they cannot vocalize it. But, again, communication is key, and you can practice it with your child. Pictures, signs, communication devices such as tablets with communication software

-Make sure you set up a "safe" area for your child, where he can go when he is upset or overwhelmed by events around him. It could be his room or a specific corner of the house. It is a good idea to let your child know that you will always be there for them whenever they need you.

Often a hiding place like a tent can help to shut the world out around them. There are "body socks" that are like a body tent made from stretchy material that lets your child check out a bit once inside it. The tight stretchy fabric also offers a sensory calming pressure on their body. We used it on air planes when things could get a bit overstimulating and we had to remain in our seats. It worked wonders.

If you are concerned about your child's behavior and social interactions, it is best to get an expert opinion. However, if you have done so already and the diagnosis was autism, you must start the treatment right away. Hopefully you are able to connect quickly with service providers and in the meantime reading up on the subject can give a lot of insight.

Theories about the Cause of Autism

Autism spectrum disorder is a neurobiological disorder. Neurobiological terms relating to autism include genetic and neuroimaging abnormalities and neurodevelopmental features. This, in turn, is closely linked to the abnormal development of the brain that affects many areas of functioning, including self-regulation, communication and social interaction. The research on this disorder combines molecular biology testing and developmental studies looking at brain structures in living individuals with autism.

There are different forms of autism, and this is why physicians need to be able to make a specific diagnosis. This can be done through medical history, physical exam and developmental screening tools (such as the Early Start Screening test) which evaluate a child's level of development from birth until around six years of age. However, even after this diagnosis, it may not be clear what caused the condition.

Chapter Two

Effects on education and academic performance in children with ASD

Children with ASD may have difficulty in their social, emotional and communication development, as well as in their academic performance.

There is often a concern about their academic performance for the following reasons:

The most significant concern is the impact of ASD on academic performance, particularly at school age. This impacts the quality of life of children with ASD, their parents and educators. Parents must understand how ASD affects children's learning and educational outcomes, how to support their children and how to help them develop as they progress through school. It is also important that they understand how they can help their child succeed and develop into a happy, engaged member of society.

Educational outcomes are always the product of a complex set of factors influenced by several factors. The most significant factors include the following:

Some schools and teachers may not realize how parents and service providers of the child perceive his abilities. Some parents may decide to enroll their child a year later. This, in turn, impacts how well they can cope in school and at home, which is a major factor when considering the quality of life for the child and family and, ultimately, the school.

On the other hand, home and family factors could impact children's academic performance. These include:

"In most countries of the world, a person's intellectual level is measured in terms of the degree of an individual's achievement in academic studies and results. Academic levels are usually described as follows:

Most parents feel that their child is receiving sufficient support to help them achieve at school, but the worry remains that their child is struggling academically.

Educational support is important to help children achieve at school and to support their home learning styles. In North America every child has the right to attend a public school. Inclusion is a very big factor and Educational Assistants and teachers alike will accommodate the child's learning abilities and modify the curriculum accordingly. This impacts the child to feel more confident about themselves and their ability to succeed in school. Everybody learns differently is the message and all children at school, whether on the spectrum or not, benefits from that way of learning.

Schools are being asked to implement new programming to support children with all kinds of special needs and it could be that these programs are more intensive than what was previously expected from schools. These changes, however, reflect the increasing understanding of what children with ASD need to succeed at school and in life.

Children with ASD will continue to have the same opportunities in school than their peers. However, some schools are now starting to provide extra educational support for children with ASD, which include:

For example, in Ontario, Canada, a program called **"The Learning Way"** effectively improves children's reading and math skills. Research from this program shows that it may be able to help students with ASD achieve academic success.

A study by the Woodside School District, New York, found 95% of students showed positive outcomes after implementing this program. However, these programs have not been applied universally, and there remains a desire for more research on similar methods of educating children with ASD.

A parent's desire to help can mean focusing on their child's learning instead of other activities in which the child participates. For example, some children with ASD may take longer than other children to develop reading and writing skills.

Some parents may focus on their child's reading and writing skills, as well as their educational performance, at the exclusion of other areas of the child's life. In my opinion it is best to work hand in hand with the school. In the younger grades teachers will send home books for what is called a home reading program. This is a wonderful opportunity to sit with your child and do some reading together. I strongly believe that a child's social emotional development is way more important than the academic development. When they start getting better with social interaction due to more exposure to other kids at school, they often pickup academics easier as well. It is important to participate in other activities at home with your children as it takes so much out of them to at school. They have to work much harder in achieving academic success and also being exposed to social interactions for a prolonged time.

Children with ASD who receive the right support at school can achieve academically. In North America typically children with ASD are mainstreamed to ensure that they are included in a wider range of activities. This will improve their social and life skills.

Main Types of Disability Support for Students with ASD in Public Education in the United States and Canada

In Canada, the different Territories have different funding for children with ASD. For example, British Columbia has funding for children with ASD to use for their development until they are 6 years old, then the funding drops to a third of the original amount until 19 years. The funding is monitored and has to be used for service providers, equipment and respite if applicable.

We went to a pediatric therapy center where we started to receive services from behavioral therapists, speech therapists, occupational therapists and early childhood interventionists. The therapists work out a program suited for the child and his level of development, and the interventionists implement the suggested therapy. I always stayed during the sessions to educate myself.

On the days we didn't have therapy, I would do the programs with my son at home to get him up to master his programs more quickly. It is essential to start intervention as early as possible; time is crucial. Once he mastered an activity/program, we went on to the next step. The programs were designed to start with the easiest task of learning a new skill and moving up from there. I cannot say enough about how important those early interventions were for my child's development.

In countries where the population is struggling with a declining quality of life, an increase in the number of people with autism spectrum disorders (ASD) is often seen. However, increased prevalence also increases the burden on families, caregivers, educators and communities because of the frequency of special education programs. Therefore, effective strategies are needed to bring people with ASD into mainstream settings and improve their functioning in meaningful ways.

In the U.S., at least 5% of children are considered to have ASD. There are an estimated 2.5 million people with autism in the United States, according to calculated data from 2016, and it is said that this number is still growing.

Students with ASD experience difficulty across many areas of their lives, including social interaction and communication skills, as well as restricted interests and repetitive behaviors.

The U.S. Administration on Intellectual and Developmental Disabilities defines learning disabilities as cognitive issues that can interfere with effective learning or cause people to feel overwhelmed by their academic work. These issues can include difficulties with processing information and understanding what they read, as well as having difficulties with performing mathematical calculations.

Learning disabilities affect over 10 million children, according to the U.S. Department of Education and the U.S. Department of Health and Human Services (DHHS). Learning disabilities can cause a child difficulty at school without being formally diagnosed. As a result, students cannot obtain the resources they need to learn effectively.

Students with learning disabilities can also be misdiagnosed with autism causing further frustration for parents and students. Unfortunately, many of these children are being missed by pediatricians and school nurses who did not suspect their child had a learning disability due to their age or developmental level.

Many parents feel overwhelmed by the demands placed on them as parents of children in special education programs that include speech therapy, physical therapy, occupational therapy, vision therapy and more. In addition, parents often wish for more access to help for their children in the classroom, including assistance with language and speech issues.

It is essential for the treatment of autism that professionals and educators coordinate a range of services to address the variety of treatments necessary for each individual. For example, children with ASD are more likely to exhibit self-injurious behaviors (SIB).

As a result, behavior analysts and teachers need to work together to create interventions that will decrease these types of behaviors by reinforcing appropriate behaviors. Current models of behavioral therapy in special education settings include intensive behavioral intervention (IBI), functional behavioral assessment (FBA), and positive behavior support (PBS). Each model has different components related specifically to autism.

A Brief History of Special Education Laws in North America

In Canada, students with ASD are being diagnosed more often and at a younger age. As a result, schools are increasingly enrolling young students who were previously un-served. These students require specialized teaching techniques to meet their needs and there have been significant advances in the education of children with special needs in the last few decades. With the prevalence of autism spectrum disorder (ASD) rising, many organizations are beginning to develop services and organizations that focus on assisting individuals with autism and their families. In addition, many of these organizations seek to advocate for individuals with ASD by providing them with educational materials, lobbying government officials on behalf of those with autism, and giving families a voice in society.

Autism is a journey I never planned, but I sure do love my tour guide

Chapter Three

Tips on Parenting Children with ASD

It can be heart-wrenching to see your child struggling to communicate and interact in the same way as their neuro-typical peers.

What can you do to make sure your child with ASD is happy, safe, and learning all that they can? Figure out what is best for the individual child, and then tailor the strategy of treatment to meet their needs.

Empowering parents enables children with ASD to be more independent and successful in school. In turn, it helps both your child as well as their classroom teacher because they will not be needing you so much during school hours. By letting go of some responsibilities like household chores, and even taking on additional tasks in the classroom like a crossing guard or playground monitor your child will be able to focus more on school work.

ASD affects a child's brain development and can make it difficult for a child to socialize, communicate, or be sensitive to others. It also makes it hard for them to control their emotions, focus on tasks and can lead to compulsive behavior and repetitive routines.

Coping with ASD requires an understanding of the condition in order to find ways to live with it most successfully. This chapter is designed as a guide for both parents and educators who have children on the spectrum.

Many people think that autism can only be diagnosed in a young person, but many children develop symptoms of autism from birth. In fact, many adults on the spectrum have been diagnosed since they were infants.

Parents of children with autism can learn more about the disorder in order to better understand their child's behavior and make them more comfortable around others. The best thing a parent can do when their child is exhibiting signs of ASD is to be supportive and open to new ideas when it comes to improving functioning and communication skills.

Developing Sensory Processing Skills to Cope with ASD

Sensory processing refers to the different ways that the brain can process sensory information. Each person's brain has its own unique sensory system, but every individual does not process all senses in the same way. Sometimes, a person's brain can't distinguish between one sense and another as easily as someone else's, leading to difficulty in certain environments.

Many times, a child on the autism spectrum has a difficult time processing sensory information. Whether it's because they haven't developed their sensibilities or because they can easily become overwhelmed by too much information, sensory processing problems for children on the autism spectrum can be very upsetting for them.

Children who do not know how to cope with over-stimulation from sensory input will find it hard to focus and participate in common activities like sports and school. They may seem out-of-touch with their own bodies and their surroundings, which can lead to compulsive behaviors.

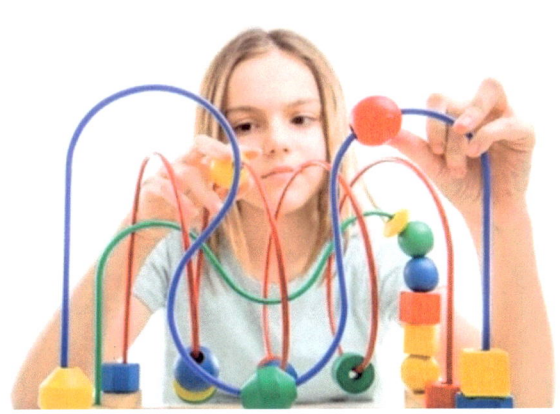

But sensory processing difficulties can be managed with the help of a special education program at school and getting services from a specialized Occupational Therapist on techniques for parents to help their child cope with sensory overload. For instance, if a child's sense of touch is too acute, wearing soft clothes without tags will be more comfortable. Sometimes certain textures can be overwhelming or soothing. My son couldn't bear the textures of spaghetti in his mouth but loved the satin fabric of the couch.

Children who have trouble processing auditory information can benefit from quiet music in the classroom. For instance, music with a low volume can help a child focus on reading.

Developing Motor Skills to Cope with ASD

Motor skills refer to the way a person's body moves and performs various tasks. If a person has poor motor skills, they will find it difficult to perform repetitive movements and tasks like running or riding a bike. They may also have trouble controlling their facial expressions and find it difficult to concentrate on simple games and just sitting in one place for very long periods of time. Children who have sensory processing problems and motor skills problems are very likely to develop autism. The combination of these two problems makes it hard to learn at school because they won't be able to focus or participate in class activities like sports. They may also be out-of-touch with their bodies and may focus on certain parts of the body, like their hands instead of focusing on the entire face.

The good news is that sensory processing, motor skills, and behavioral therapy can all be improved using different techniques. These techniques are taught in special education classes at school so that a child can learn how to cope with over-stimulation and become more comfortable in new environments.

Creating an Individualized Communication Plan for ASD Children

Communication is a very important part of the human experience. Communication with other people is about learning about others and sharing experiences in order to become closer. But without proper communication skills, it's hard for people to relate to others or misunderstand each other.

Without an understanding of what others are trying to say, it can be very confusing when someone says something that doesn't make sense. This can lead to an uncomfortable situation and even create chaos in a classroom or on the playing field. It can also lead to miscommunication between parents and children, which can cause confusion at home as well.

But learning how to communicate your ideas and feelings to others can be difficult for kids on the autism spectrum. The good news is that there are many techniques for helping children with autism learn how to communicate. There are a lot of different ways to communicate and when the language isn't developed kids refer to touch, sounds and certain behaviors to communicate their needs. A much more organized and streamlined way is sign language, communication output devices which are these days in form of a tablet with a speech program installed.

Using an AAC device like a communication book is another way a child can be able to communicate their wants or needs.

It allows them to choose from a variety of pictures that show what they want to say. It also allows them to find ways of saying things when they don't know the exact word or have a hard time pronouncing verbally.

Sometimes people might be saying one thing but mean something else entirely. This is called "pragmatic language." It can be very confusing for children on the autism spectrum because it can cause a lot of misunderstandings and hurt feelings. However, if you teach your child pragmatics along with social rules in hopes of minimizing behavior problems, this will help improve his ability to interact with others and take cues from his environment.

Teaching children with ASD how to understand pragmatic language skills, like understanding whether people are being sarcastic when they say one thing, can help them when they're interacting with other people.

Other Communication Skills that Can Help Alleviate Behavioral Issues.

There are many things that can be taught at home to help a child on the autism spectrum become more comfortable in different settings. For instance, if they find certain sounds stimulating like tapping or shouting, soft music or TV programs can be used to reduce these noises in the home and make their environment more comfortable.

Understanding how to give a proper greeting is just as important. If a person greets someone with a hug or kiss, the person being greeted may be unprepared and uncomfortable with this kind of physical contact. But thankfully, there are many ways to approach social situations and learn how to greet others in an appropriate manner.

The good news is that there are many therapies and techniques that can be used to help children on the autism spectrum adjust to different situations. While they may always have difficulty socializing, their environment can provide them with ways of making relationships better and helping them talk more comfortably with their peers at school, family members at home and in general public. It's also likely that they'll need additional help at home in order to become more comfortable and focused in the classroom. Learning how to cope with sensory processing and motor skills problems can have an enormous impact on how well they do at school and being accepted by their peers.

Here are some additional ways that you can empower your child:

1. Encourage Independence and Self-Determination – Children with ASD may feel overwhelmed by too much pressure and stress which could cause them to feel trapped and confused. You could help them manage this by establishing a routine of "homework" or daily activities and then being rewarded for a job well done. This way they will learn to start caring for themselves and make their own choices. As your child grows older, he will begin to become more independent and autonomous in his daily tasks.

2. Teach your child to identify and express emotions. Children with ASD may have trouble understanding their own emotions or those of others. So, it is very important that you teach your child the basic emotions

such as "happy, sad, mad, glad and scared" by using stories or pictures in a visual format.

3. Help your child learn about the world around them. Each parent will need to assess their unique situation and find an appropriate teaching method for their child's specific needs and abilities. Always include your child in the learning process to give them a sense of belonging within the family and group setting they are part of.

Many children with ASD have limited knowledge about the world around them such as different countries, capital cities, languages, cultural differences and so on. To help your child learn more about the world you live in, you could take them on outings to new places so they can experience new environments.

4. Encourage your child to be more physically active and increase their time spent outdoors. Children who are on the spectrum may be more comfortable interacting within their own set of familiar surroundings rather than venturing into a new environment where they do not feel safe or comfortable. Parents can help encourage their children by stimulating them with outside activities such as going on a nature walk or playing hide and seek in the park at the end of the day. Most kids love the swimming pool and fast water slides are stimulating for them, if they can tolerate the noise level.

5. Strengthen the family bond by doing family tasks together. You could involve your child in household chores by helping them to clean their

rooms, taking out the trash, or setting the table at dinner time. This will help your child feel like a part of your family and recognize the importance of contributing to their own home and feel comfortable about being a member of their own community.

These tips on parenting children with ASD can help you empower your child to be more independent and make good choices.

Some kids on the spectrum have a hard time looking at the speaker. With non-verbal kids that's a problem as they have to look at your mouth to see how a word is spoken. I sometimes used a mirror or an iPad in selfie mode to have the child look into and see my face through the device. They had a much easier time to look at my face that way and were able to watch me saying a word. They could then watch themselves copying me.

Chapter Four

School and Learning- Getting the Right Education for a Child

Schools are an important part of the day of children with autism. Depending on the level of their needs they most likely will have special help in school situations. Although they can learn in many of the same ways as children who do not have autism, they have trouble doing so. This is because they often think and learn in different ways than other children, and they have trouble with some of the skills that are taught in school.

The help that a child needs will vary from one child to another. Some require help for the whole day on a one on one situation, while others need help for curtained learning times during the day. The kinds of help needed also vary a great deal from one skill to another. It is best for a child to be helped by someone who knows about both autism and education like an Educational Assistant.

Parents of autistic children should find out as much as they can about the school situation before their child enters kindergarten or elementary school. Many different kinds of schools provide education for children with autism, including private and public schools, special schools and classes in regular schools. It is best for parents to visit several kinds of schools before deciding which one will help their child the most.

When children with autism enter school, they may need special help in many ways. A parent approach to teaching usually works best, but when a more structured method is needed, it should be used. The kinds of help that children with autism will need will depend on their overall level of ability in the areas of learning and self-advocacy.

Schools have a significant role in helping children with autism learn better. While some schools provide a very good environment for a child with autism, others may not. Parents should be invited to a team based meeting to create an Individual Educational Plan (IEP) where it will be determined how the child's education will be supported in the best possible way matched to his abilities and strengths. The school based team can consist of a range of people including the principal, Integration Support Teacher, Educational Assistant, classroom teacher, Speech Pathologist, Occupational Therapist and sometimes an outside person like the child's psychologist or an out of school service provider. Here it can be talked about whether any problems are occurring, the kinds of problems that are happening, and the kinds of help that is needed. Parents play a big role in those meetings and have the right to make themselves heard and to be a part of their child's learning at school.

Learning

We were lucky enough to live in North America where inclusion is really big and has been for many years. Europe is still a bit behind in succeeding in that matter but there is a change in the right direction there, too.

I really feel very strongly about the fact that children with special needs attending public school is beneficial not only for them but for neuro-typical children as well. The children become aware that people learn at different paces and that there might be kids who have higher needs than themselves.

They learn how to be compassionate and create empathy. In my years as an Educational Assistant I found myself often in situations that left me in absolute awe of what young kids are capable of doing when it comes to helping someone who might be struggling.

Milo, Grade 1 and nonverbal, expressed his discomfort by making a very distinct noise. Only a few weeks into the school year his classmates noticed that he was uncomfortable when he made those noises. They knew that rubbing his back or hold his hand settled him and I was never short of volunteers. Don't get me wrong, I never asked any of them to comfort him, they stepped up all by themselves and enjoyed being kind and making a difference in the day of their classmate.

In return Milo taught the kids compassion, empathy and kindness, which is something we can't teach kids unless they experience it. He went on and had the same core friends for the rest of his time in Elementary School and I truly believe his peers are smarter, kinder and compassionate people because of what they learned from Milo.

For literacy in my experience kids with ASD seem to have an easier time to learn in full words or phrases. Letter recognition is possible, however the understanding that those letters sounded out will create a word is a very hard concept. Therefore, flashcards or reading books with phrases that repeat themselves are great resource to start with.

In my work I would take pictures of familiar things in the child's life, i.e. Family members, favorite stuffie or toy, favorite activities etc. and pair each picture with a corresponding short sentence, i.e. *here is Mom, I love my Teddy* etc. The task is that the child will match the picture with the corresponding sentence. You can start with two pictures and one sentence. When the child masters this task you can switch to one picture and two sentences, then 3 and so on. You can expand accordingly until the child will independently match the right sentences to the right picture.

Most flashcards available will have the picture and the word on one card. Having the word and the picture separated will challenge the child to find the right word independently. I liked to make my own flash cards for my students. I start with two pictures and one word, i.e. a dog and a dolphin picture and the word dog and have the child find the right word. After he has mastered that task you can go from one picture to two words, then 3 words etc.

Since my student loved books I created a book about his day at school. I paired the pictures with a 3-4-word sentence to describe the picture. Every picture has to have a meaning to the student to make it interesting enough for him to look at it. His lunch kit, him washing hands, his favorite chair at school, his Mom picking him up etc.

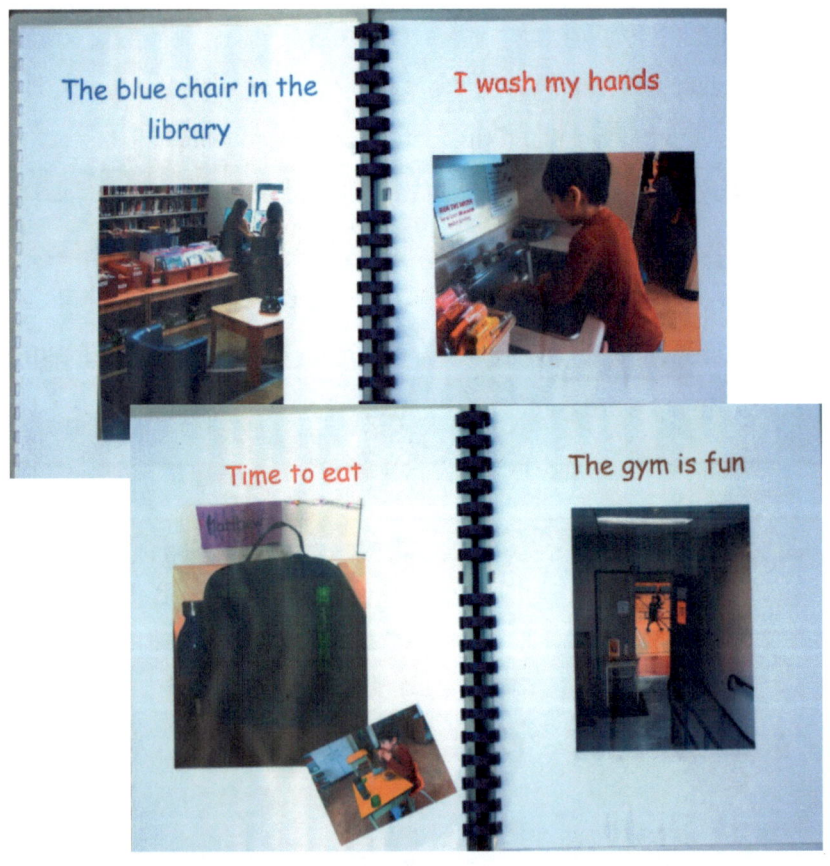

Visuals:

The majority of people in the world are visual learners. When we see something, it is easier to follow or remember then hearing or reading about it. I would say that for young kids with ASD visuals are a life saver.

Transitions are usually a trigger for behavior. To make it easier on child and parent a visual schedule is very helpful. It can have only 2 pictures as in a "first - then" approach or if your child can handle it there could be the whole morning or day laid out.

With my child pictures of the actual subjects were better to comprehend, i.e. a picture of my car when we were going out, a picture of the actual pool we were going to, a picture of grandma if we were to visit there today etc. However, there is a program available called PECS (picture exchange program system) that stores thousands of pictures that can be downloaded and printed into little cards.

I created social stories with pictures for my child when I wanted him to stop a certain behavior. For Example if I wanted him to stop throwing objects I would show a picture where someone throws something with a sad emoji next to it and the next page shows the object being handled appropriately with a smiley face. The last page would show an object that is expected to be thrown like a ball or a Frisbee to let him know that there will be still opportunities to throw something but in an expected kind of way.

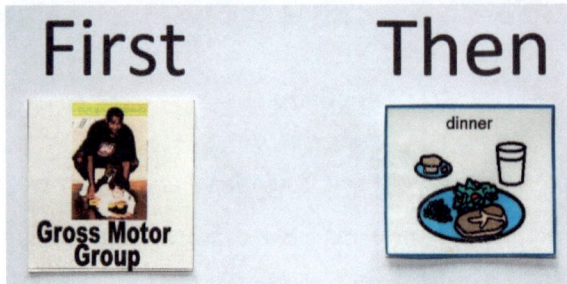

Example of a short visual schedule, suitable when first introducing a schedule

If the child is getting used to a schedule it can be expanded

This approach is helpful when there is an expectation or a less preferred activity. It makes the child aware that something they prefer is following and it will make her more tolerable to take on the task before.

At age 4 my son was very fixated on a special pair of pajamas. He wanted to wear them every night but they had to go in the laundry (a concept a 4-year-old doesn't understand at the best of times)! Meltdowns every time the pajamas were in the laundry. Eventually I noticed that he was fine when I told him the pajamas are in the wash and he was fine when I opened up the drawer as well. But he was getting upset the minute he took a look inside the drawer.

It seemed to me that he was agitated at the fact that he didn't know ahead of time whether they were there or not, even though I told him but kids with ASD often experience what is called an auditory processing disorder (a delay in processing time of instructions or verbal commands) I printed one picture of his pajamas and one of a washing machine and stuck them with Velcro on the drawer of his dresser.

I explained to him that whenever he sees the picture with the pajamas on the drawer it means that they will be inside the drawer and every time he sees the washer it means that they are in the laundry and therefore not inside the drawer. Low and behold that did the trick! It wasn't the pajamas; it was the anticipation and then not being in the know.

After a few weeks he didn't even care anymore about those pajamas and that right after I hunted down an identical pair in a size bigger! I used visuals all over my house, it will truly make life easier for you and your child.

How to Cope with Behaviors for the Child in the School

1. The teachers must understand that children with autism also want to learn. They may not be able to communicate as well as other children, but they can still learn. Teaching staff should find out whether there are any extra programs for children with autism being offered at the school and follow these suggestions if there are.

2. In order to create a plan for students with autism within the school, educators need to first understand how students who are on the spectrum learn differently from other students. Under such a plan, teaching staff must understand the different teaching strategies needed to teach students with special needs such as autism. This will ensure

that the student receives an adequate education and the teachers are able to get consistent ratings on their performance reviews.

3. Due to their different learning styles and communication needs, many students with autism spectrum disorders have trouble adjusting socially within the classroom. This can make it difficult for their teachers to communicate effectively with them and give them the help that they need. The way to go about this is to develop strategies to help these students succeed socially within the classroom.

One way that teaching staff can learn how to socially integrate students with autism spectrum disorders is to take an active role in their education. It is important that parents and educators work together to help their children succeed socially within the classroom. Being actively involved in the education of children with autism can help teaching staff develop a better understanding of how to motivate and teach the children.

Another important part of this plan is to work with other students who do not have an autism spectrum disorder as well. Some old school teachers may still be used to teaching students with autism separately, but this can make it difficult for the other students in the class because they do not receive any social interaction with them. It is very important for teachers to learn how to teach all students in the class in order to help them succeed socially.

Some of these skills include the following:

Communication skills: Being able to communicate effectively with others is one of the most important aspects of school and helps students learn and grow socially.

Leadership skills: Leadership skills are extremely important for all children in school, but those with special needs often face extra challenges when it comes to gaining this skill. For this reason, it is important for teachers and parents to develop a plan for teaching the child leadership skills as well.

Social skills: Social skills are also an important part of education for all children, but those whom have special needs often face extra challenges when learning these skills. For this reason, parents and teachers should work together to develop a program that specifically develops the social skills of students with special needs who are participating in school.

In order for children with autism spectrum disorders to progress socially within the classroom without being overwhelmed or frustrated, it is essential for teaching staff and parents to create a specialized individual education plan that allows them to be successful. Without this collaboration, children will either become discouraged or become frustrated, or they may be unable to express their concerns or needs. Therefore, the teaching staff is responsible for creating a plan that helps children succeed within the classroom by providing them with all of the necessary support.

Chapter Five

The Transition to Adulthood

Transition plans that may be needed when your child becomes of age. As a parent of someone with ASD, there are many fears and unknowns that come with raising a child on the spectrum. As the children grow, their peers will change, they may struggle to adapt socially, they may struggle in school, and their surroundings. So now what do parents have to prepare for? How can we raise children with autism successfully as they age into adulthood?

In this chapter, we discuss how parents can prepare for the transition from childhood to adulthood through considering some coping strategies that help get through day-to-day challenges so your child can live life more independently and find success in their future endeavors.

Transition to adulthood is a big one, and it is not something that should be taken lightly. No matter how prepared we have been there are always going to be surprises.

Here are some helpful ways to help your child's transitioning:

Finding a support group, or joining an Autism parenting forum that offers support with other parents who have been through similar situations can help tremendously in times of need.

The parents in these groups tend to look out for each other better than on-line forums because they are able to give advice based on their personal experience and what they have experienced with their child. This can save you quite a bit of time and money as it means that you do not have to research how to manage these transitions.

As your child grows, they will also grow more independent and self-sufficient. This is when some parents may feel uneasy with their children growing up. This is normal and should not be a cause of concern. This means that you need to reinforce your child's independence in a positive way while they still need you to guide them through the process. If your child wants to do things on their own, they should be allowed to do it when they are old enough to understand the risks involved in certain activities.

Kids can become more independent at any time, which is why support groups have been set up so parents can find comfort in discussion of their children's growth into adulthood with other parents who have had similar experiences.

Parents should also be prepared for some difficulties in the later stage of life, as the school system is changing, along with the different ways we can adapt to new and improved technology.

Having a spouse or partner or a good friend or family member that shares your anxiety about how your child may cope is also important.

Your spouse/partner/friend/family member will help you cope when you are feeling anxious as they can understand your worries better than anyone else. Having someone who understands what you may be going through can provide comfort and reassurance that having any good advice to help guide you through these unknowns; it might feel like you are taking control of everything but if parents are able to express themselves they will find their own strength that they may not have even known existed before.

For parents that have children with ASD having a routine to support your child and to make them feel less alone is important. This can also be extremely helpful for your child as routine helps in everything from emotion regulation, planning future events and reducing stress and anxiety. However, you may want to do things differently than parents of neuro-typical children would if your child does not like certain routines or if you are unsure about how these will affect them.

Letting your child make choices and try things on their own helps their development as well as making them more independent.

If they choose not to eat vegetables, they should still be allowed to enjoy other aspects of life like playing computer games as long as they are safe.

This can also help them to tone down the anxious feelings that they may feel as a result of a routine. Having a good controlled routine will help your child feel secure and is also necessary for their progress in growing into adulthood.

As parents, we put billions of hours into teaching our children how to do things for themselves because we want them to be independent when it comes time for them to move out or work on their own. So, spending the time and energy now teaching these skills will help you both once they are old enough.

Some children may feel unfulfilled in their role in society and not know what they should be doing with their lives. This is a difficult issue as children will grow up to be adults and you will want them to do well. But it is often difficult to know how they should go about making this transition without any assistance from professionals.

However, there are ways that parents can help prepare them for the future. For example, when your child reaches age 18 you may notice that he/she has an interest in another career path than he did when he was younger. There are many different careers out there for adults with ASD; these include things like computer programmers or engineers for example.

So, it is important to actively encourage your child to find out more about these options and fill out the required paperwork. But remember, it is not a requirement. Parents can let their children know that they are not being forced into any particular industry just because they are 18, but rather because this is something that they would like to do.

Another way to help your child cope with these unknowns that come with adulthood is having a support system in place in case he/she needs some assistance getting through tough periods in life.

This support system can take many forms such as having a family member or friend who has experience with ASD, or finding a support group created by parents of adult children with ASD. Having a support group for parents that have children with ASD can be a great way to understand the concerns of other parents, as well as learn what you may need to do in order to get the professionals involved.

It is also important to be prepared for your child's future, by knowing what your child's needs are at different ages and stages in life. This includes things like adolescence and adulthood; this means that you need to know when you need to talk with your child's teachers about their anxiety and fears as they may not be able to express these emotions themselves. You should also have a plan of action if your child reaches adulthood and cannot take care of themselves or their own affairs.

These are smaller issues that parents may not have thought about before, or don't even know how to approach. It is important to be prepared for these situations so that your child can transition into adulthood without any problems.

One of the biggest fears when it comes to raising a child with autism is how they will cope on their own. Will they be able to make friends? How will they manage their independence? What worries after college?

For some families, this is not that big of a concern because they either don't want to raise an independent teenager or their children are too high needs and therefore dependent on them that moving out is not an option. However, for other families having a plan is important; it may not be something that you think about but it is important to keep your child's progress in mind.

When you think about where your child will be in the future, no one likes to think about their children having any problems once they are 'grown up'. However, there are plans that need to be made and information that needs to be gathered. For example, when thinking about how your child will manage their own affairs in the future, there should be a plan written out with all of the necessary information included. This will be useful for any potential problems that might occur.

As a parent, it is important to know what your child wants out of their future if they can communicate or understand your questions. This can be found in the form of journals, drawings or through conversation. However, this information may not always be available depending on the child's level of understanding and communicating his needs and wants.

In some cases professional might be able to help you find answers to these questions by speaking with your child; even if they aren't able to speak for themselves.

This helps you to set up a plan based around their interests and the thoughts that they want expressed down the road. This is especially important when thinking about things like financial matters or where they want to live.

It is also important to keep your child's best interests in mind, if they have expressed a desire to move into one of these forms of living after close relatives have passed on. Having a plan in place because it shows your child that you are thinking about their future. You are also showing them that you understand their feelings and that you care enough about them to make this happen.

Another plan for your child is creating a social support group for them in the future.

Finding teenagers or adults with ASD already in the working world may help ease the transition into adulthood. Your child can benefit greatly from having someone who understands how they feel and can offer them advice as well as support. This is especially important in your community as it can be difficult to find the right fit for your child.

As a parent, it is always hard to think about your child leaving the home. This is especially true if they have autism because it can be hard to imagine them being able to cope on their own. It is important that you keep your child's best interests in mind. You will want to take advantage of every opportunity that they are offered; whether it be something like school or social programs in your community. They may be some of the only chances you have to get them used to working with people their own age or living on their own.

Chapter Six

Helping a Child with ASD

Each day, new research surfaces about the condition, broadening our awareness and understanding of how to cope with a child on the autism spectrum. Our kids on the spectrum are not just our children, they are a part of their whole community. When we invite them to be a part of the world, we make it smaller and better-connected.

Children with autism deserve the same standards as other children in education. They need access to arts and crafts that provide an outlet for creativity; they need help developing social skills with other children in inclusive environments; they need help understanding what is happening to them in school and at home; they need reasonable accommodations for sensory sensitivities or disabilities like epilepsy or ADHD so that no one is left behind. All these things can make a huge difference for your child.

People with ASD have social and communication difficulties, particularly with language and pragmatics, but their difficulties in these areas may be overcome to various degrees as they develop. Many people with autism also have repetitive behaviors like rocking back and forth or flapping their hands. The brains of people on the autism spectrum work differently than those without it, so it's no surprise that some difficulties can be experienced because of this difference.

Helping a child with ASD can be challenging. Every day you will be faced with new situations, finding the right words, and deciphering correct responses. It can be exhausting, frustrating and isolating. It can be overwhelming and discouraging. ASD affects every area of their life and affects them in different ways. There are cases where children with ASD don't make eye contact, speak hardly at all or they don't seem interested in playing and won't use their toys appropriately.

There are an enormous array of resources out there that can help calm the waters. With the internet a whole new world opened up for those searching for a likeminded community, groups, blogs, books etc., on top of local service providers of different professions.

ASD affects each child differently. The good news is that despite their differences, most children with ASD can learn and develop and there are things you can do to help them along the way!

Being on the autism spectrum requires a lot of support. In any case it involves extra help from parents, teaching staff and therapists. Most importantly it requires patience. Children with ASD may not be able to understand the world in quite the same way that other kids do.

Early Intervention and Therapies

Practitioner Services:

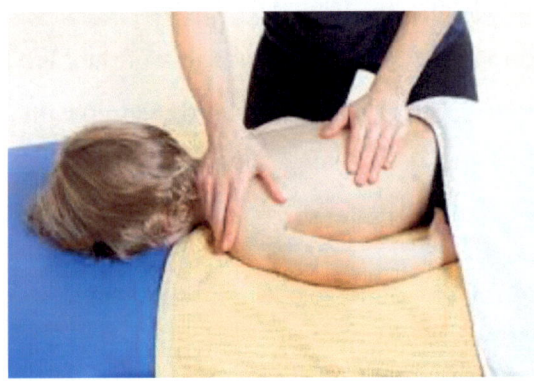

Chiropractic can be very helpful. The central nervous system of kids with ASD is often in high arousal and a chiropractic treatment can have a calming effect on the nervous system. Chiropractic helps to release muscle tension and help facilitate the body's self-repair process. The relationship between the body and mind is a key to helping control behavioral problems and neurological disorders.

Naturopathic treatments can help as well if that is something you want to consider for your child. Naturopathic treatment uses natural remedies to help the body heal itself. It embraces many therapies,

Including herbs, massage, acupuncture, exercise, and nutritional counseling.

It was very helpful for us and we always had treatments that were fully tailored to my son's unique needs. Naturopathic medicine addresses the entire system of the body and is more holistic than conventional medicine.

Neurofeedback done by a certified practitioner made a big difference for my son's focus at school and his anxiety. It is a type of biofeedback that helps to harmonize the brain waves naturally without medications.

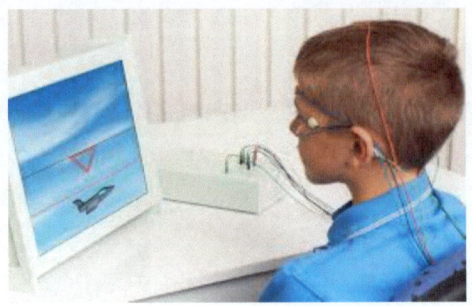

During the neurofeedback sessions the brain learns how to bring abnormally fast or slow brain waves into the normal range.

Therapies:

Occupational Therapy:

My son at age 5 asked me if I could sit in front of him on the couch and lean my body against his. I was confused and worried at first but then I learned that children with neurological disorders often crave deep pressure to calm their nervous system.

Occupational therapy works to improve the life skills and vocational path of persons. OT's are working on gross and fine motor skills. Activities like taking small objects and sort them into jars with tweezers (fine motor skills) or developing large muscle groups, i.e. to be able to use both feet when walking stairs or gain better muscle control in their hands so they can tie their shoes.

Some OTs are specifically trained to address feeding and swallowing challenges in kids with autism. They can evaluate the particular issue a child is experiencing and provide treatment plans for improving feeding-related challenges. Feeding therapy introduces new foods to picky eaters in a safe, play-based environment.

This method is based on research that indicates feeding difficulties are almost always due to oral motor delays and/ or difficulties with sensory processing. They consider the normal developmental stages of eating and build up children's skills in these areas so that they can manage a wide variety of foods.

In our case the OT created a plan of all my son's preferred foods and modified it ever so slightly to expand his palate. As parents we know all too well that in the end the child controls what goes in and out of their bodies so sometimes it will take a while but it could be a game changer especially if there are food sensitivities involved.

Occupational Therapy helps children develop fine motor skills and self-help skills such as feeding and dressing themselves. Physical Therapists can help children with walking problems. Special education classes can help children develop social skills, language and academic skills through interaction with their peers.

Speech Therapy:

The speech-language pathologist is involved with assessment and development of programs to treat speech and language delays. This may include verbal and non-verbal receptive and expressive language as well as articulation disorders.

I worked with a boy named Leo when he was 6 and in Grade 1. For his entire Kindergarten year, he was noncompliant to come inside the school. Most of his days were spent outside and only for lunch he would agree to come in.

Our focus was to keep him included with his peers in the classroom which proofed to be a very hard task for him and for me as his Educational Assistant. At the time he had a private Speech Pathologist and they have been trying for a while to get him to speak. He was completely nonverbal. The Speech Path got him acquainted with a speech program downloaded on a tablet that was working as a voice output device. He pressed a picture with an apple and his tablet would say "apple".

It took him only a few weeks to get comfortable with it and soon was able to output 3-word sentences in a short period of time. Within 6 months at school and with the help of the speech software he learned to communicate his needs and wants. He started to love his table jobs and learning materials in the classroom. By the end of Grade 1 he knew the letters of the alphabet, numbers up to 30 and we were on our way to get him potty trained.

The success was clearly due to the fact that he realized how much value it has to be able to communicate with the people around him. He finally was willing to participate as a more active part in his social environment because it lowered his frustration levels and finally people understood what he was saying, in his own unique way.

Other kids with ASD are verbal but do not use their words to communicate. Often there will be a repetition of the same phrase or a full recital of their favorite scene from a movie or a show they watched but when asked a yes or no question they won't be able to answer reliably.

Speech therapy assesses and treats speech disorders and communication problems. It helps people develop skills like comprehension, clarity, voice, fluency and sound production. Speech therapy can treat childhood speech disorders. Speech Therapy is helpful when children have speech delays or have selective mutism which is an inability to speak in certain situations.

Psychological therapy:

Cognitive Behavioral Therapy (CBT) teaches people with ASD to recognize and express feelings more effectively, improve their moods and behavior, learn to regulate their actions, and develop new social skills.

These therapies help people with ASD increase their awareness of how they think, feel and behave to give them the tools needed to manage their life better. These therapies have been shown to help reduce symptoms in people with ASD who have depression and anxiety as well as improve general functioning.

Behavioral therapy:

Behavioral therapy is used to show which of the following types of behaviors are bothering the person with autism. Behavioral therapy will identify which behavior the therapist wants to block. It also helps a person learn how to solve problems by making them aware of their own emotions, thoughts, and feelings. It continues with behavioral treatments that help improve social skills in children with autism.

For most people with autism, the key aspect of treatment is behavioral therapy. Most practitioners agree that behavioral therapy will help reduce the severity of symptoms in children who have autism. Although it is not a cure for autism, it can improve many areas such as cognitive development and social abilities.

Parents and educators can use behavior modification techniques such as positive reinforcement techniques along with behavioral techniques when teaching new behaviors or thinking patterns in children with ASD. The principle behind positive reinforcement is that the response you give a child when they do something right will make them want to repeat it again.

Behavior modification techniques are used to solve problems in children with autism by decreasing or eliminating unwanted behaviors. One of the most common types of behavior modification techniques is known as operant conditioning. Operant conditioning involves activities that teach new behaviors and thoughts. This type of behavioral therapy can help children learn to control their emotions or attention, by reinforcing the correct behaviors and ignoring the incorrect ones.

In most cases, cognitive behavioral therapy is used along with behavior therapy to teach a child coping mechanisms for living and functioning without becoming overwhelmed. For example, it can be implemented as part of an individual's treatment plan, as part of an educational setting, or in both settings to help people deal with multiple challenges at once (i.e. learning a different language while also attending school).

My son was especially enjoying equestrian behavioral therapy. The goal is to use horses for behavioral development of the child. The child had to make sure the horse was comfortable before he could mount. That was done in the same routine every time. First look at the horse's face, does he look relaxed? Check the hoofs, most likely they need to be cleaned before riding the horse so his feed won't hurt him. Help carry the heavy saddle and put it on the horse, tighten the straps etc. This routine taught my child empathy, which he lacked before we started the equestrian program. It was such an amazing experience and we stayed with this program for 6 years. To give the child the opportunity to bond with the horse the kids could ride bareback. We also worked on gaining awareness of ones surroundings. The instructor would hide large cardboard shapes along the riding path. They would be up high or somewhere low or behind bushes and my son had the same shapes with him on the horse and had to find the matching shapes in his surroundings. The improvement of his spatial awareness was immense.

How Parents Can Help Children with ASD

It's important for you to provide support when meeting your child's needs. Here are some basic things parents can do to help their kids:

– Explain the rules and what expected behavior looks like. Then, enforce consequences for unexpected behavior whatever that might look like in your family unit. I did not use time outs for my son as he didn't respond to it very well. I found it way more beneficial when I removed myself from the room. That way we could both get a break and take a breather. High praise for expected behavior and really overemphasize it so the child feels good about herself. Teach your children the rules and it will help them successfully interact with others and socialize as they grow up. Don't be overprotective.

– Make sure your child socializes with other kids to help him learn by watching and copying them and how to express emotions accordingly.

– Work together with your School's teaching staff to be sure that you understand your child's academic needs, behavior, and social skills. Accept Guidance and attend any meeting they will offer to you (or ask for a meeting when you feel it's needed)

– Take advantage of the support network that is available to you – there are great websites out there providing information from parent experts.

– Be a resource and willing to share your knowledge in the community. Share your experience with other parents, offer to do things with your child that are helpful, like reading aloud together and practicing social skills.

-You can roll play certain situations to make it more visual for your child. My husband and I always role played tricky social situations that occurred. We would play out how it actually went and then played out how it should have went to make our son understand what went wrong.

– Try different Strategies. Don't try "one size fits all" strategies for every situation. Try to think of what works for you and what doesn't work for you based on your child's preferences (e.g., a program that works on one day may not work on another day). Starting out with a behavioral intervention (e.g. OT, Speech Therapy) will give you the opportunity to come up with different strategies.

Chapter Seven

Helpful Tips for Parents of Children with ASD in Poverty

Your child has been diagnosed with autism spectrum disorder (ASD) and you're struggling to provide the necessities of life for both of you. You know that your child will require intense, long-term support in education, therapy and other critical needs. You may not have the resources to meet these needs yourself or you may not have any family members or friends who can help out financially either. If this is the case, don't fret as there are a number of sources for financial assistance.

Poverty affects those with autism more than any other group. Financial problems are the number one stressor for individuals with ASD as well as their family members. Children and adults with autism often require constant care, which makes it hard to make ends meet.

There are many children on the spectrum who have little or no support as they grow up. Providing that support can be tricky, but it is worth the effort because these kids can make huge leaps forward with the right amount of expert guidance and parental involvement.

The financial struggle of parents of children diagnosed with ASD in poverty is understandably very tough. Yet, there are a lot of state/provincial and family programs that can provide support. In order to be able to utilize these services and get the support you need for your child with autism, here are some helpful tips.

When looking for ways on how to provide for your child's needs, there is the option of getting on the disability program. Since autism is a recognized disability by Federal and Provincial Government in Canada and the Social Security Administration in the U.S. Applying for this program will often provide financial support needed by parents. The guidelines of the program are very simple, and you may apply for it by contacting your provincial Child and Family Services Program or the Autism Funding Unit when you live in Canada. In the U.S apply to your local Social Security Administration office and you can also contact the Autism Self Advocacy Network (ASAN) for a free consultation on how to apply for disability.

In order to become a part of government assistance programs, it is important that you contact the local social service offices to have your children be reviewed. Many programs will then provide financial aid needed with children with autism. These will also include your local clinics, as some of them provide services that can help children with autism.

There are also charities that cater to the needs of families. They offer free medical check-ups and advice, along with financial assistance. All these services can greatly relieve the financial burden of parents with children with ASD in poverty.

Financial Assistance Programs for Children with Autism in Poverty

1. Families of children with disabilities may be eligible for SSI/SSDI benefits

Social Security Disability Insurance (SSDI) and Supplemental Security Income (SSI) are government programs that support people with disabilities. To receive benefits, a child must have a medical diagnosis that meets Social Security Administration criteria and have limited income and resources. There is a 5-month waiting period for SSI and for SSDI to become effective, children must meet certain educational criteria on an IEP. To find out if your child is eligible, visit the Social Security website at socialsecurity.gov. (US)

2. There are a number of programs that provide financial assistance for families of children with special needs

There are a number of programs that provide financial assistance for families of children with special needs, as well as adults with disabilities. Federal and state/provincial governments have federally funded special needs programs that are designed to support families of children with disabilities, including hearing and visual impairments, physical disabilities, cognitive delays, autism spectrum disorders and other developmental disabilities.

3. There are special needs trusts for parents of children with special needs

There are thousands of special needs trusts that have been set up for families in need. Some of these trusts were created by organizations as a service to parents, while others were created by individuals or companies as a business expense deduction. The purpose of these trusts is to provide financial assistance to families in need. If you are in need, find out if there is a trust in your area.

4. There are autism organizations that provide financial assistance for children with autism spectrum disorder

Most autism organizations provide a number of services to families affected by ASD. Most of these organizations offer financial assistance to families in need and sometimes, the services provided by these organizations can be free or at little cost. Some of these programs include financial support for education and therapy costs as well as respite care, family counseling and other services that may be needed by your family. Organizations like Autism Speaks even provide grants and scholarships to individuals with ASD who want to pursue higher education or vocational training programs. Find out if there is an organization in your area that can provide you with assistance.

5. Go online to find out if there are grants, scholarships and other financial aid available for families of children with autism spectrum disorder

The internet has become a great resource for finding information related to everything from local services to how to apply for scholarships and grants. While many of these websites are designed to help you receive financial assistance through grants and scholarships, others may be focused on giving tips on how you can cope with ASD.

Conclusion

Autism Spectrum Disorder is a neurodevelopmental disorder that affects how a person communicates, interacts, and relates to other people. Educational support is needed because children with ASD have a different way of learning and need one on one time for their learning.

Specialized teaching methods are needed along with additional behavior support to help students learn at their own pace and eliminate frustration. Parents, if possible, should be proactive in their approach of educating their children through educational toys and/or software that promote understanding of basic concepts or other improved means. By utilizing these as well as natural learning techniques such as social stories and visual supports while also working on building a personalized IEP plan, families can work efficiently together to ensure children with ASD succeed both academically and socially.

Having said all that, the most important thing is that we are proud parents of children with ASD. Every one of them is different in their unique ways and personalities.

My son taught me how to stop every once in a while and see the world through his eyes. I loved these moments we had together when I realized that he actually tried to tell me something when he just had that outburst of disapproval. Those were the moments we both learned and appreciated each other the most. I wouldn't miss it for the world.

So if you can, watch your child and explore their world with them, they can truly show you some magical places if you let them - I promise.

Acknowledgements

Thank you to my family and friends who always believed in me more than I ever would.

My deepest gratitude to all the children on the autism spectrum, who I had the honor to get to know and cherish, for teaching me patience, compassion and to always believe.

A big thank you to Charlotte Kenny and Matthew Jung for giving me permission to use their pictures with their beautiful faces in my book.

My all-time favorite artist Beate Knippelberg for creating yet another masterpiece with my publishing logo.

To my boy Luke, who inspired me to write this book, for being who you are. If I could change anything I would change nothing. You couldn't be more perfect and I couldn't be more proud to call myself your Mom.

References

https://PECS-canada.com

Michelle Garcia Winner

https://socialthinking.com

Leslie Broun

(Webinar at Autism Awareness Centre and author of "Literacy skill Development for Students with Special Learning Needs" and "Autism Spectrum Disorder: Building Foundation Skills in Mathematics")

Diagnostics one of the most common tests used to. https://www.coursehero.com/file/p5qlkggf/Diagnostics-One-of-the-most-common-tests-used-to-determine-if-someone-is/

Choice Theory Basic Needs - brucedavenport.com.
https://brucedavenport.com/basic-needs.html

EurekAlert!
https://www.eurekalert.org/news-releases/712337

Neurosciences Deakin.

https://www.deakin.edu.au/seed/our-research/interpersonal-neurosciencesOccupational Therapy | Greater Regional.

https://www.greaterregional.org/occupational-therapy

Occupational Therapy (OT) | Autism Speaks.

https://www.autismspeaks.org/occupational-therapy-ot-0

Cleveland Scholarship: How to Apply | Ohio Department of Education.
https://education.ohio.gov/Topics/Other-Resources/Scholarships/Cleveland-Scholarship-Tutoring-Program/Cleveland-Scholarship-Tutoring-Program-How-to-Appl

Quotes

Until you have a child with special needs, you have no idea of the depth of your strength, tenacity and resourcefulness. –

There needs to be a lot more emphasis on what a child can do instead of what he cannot do. – *Temple Grandin*

A child with autism isn't ignoring you; they are simply waiting for you to enter their world. –

The strongest people are not those that show strength in front of us but those who win battles we know nothing about. –

Why fit in when you were born to stand out. – *Dr. Seuss*

When you feel overwhelmed let go and send your worries to the Universe. Allow the lightness to wash over you and trust that everything will be ok, because it has to be. – *Sylvia Schoderer Stevens*

About the Author

Sylvia Schoderer Stevens was born and lived in Bayreuth, Germany for the majority of her life until she moved to Victoria, British Columbia, Canada with her family in 2005. A former photographer by profession, Sylvia is to date working as an Educational Assistant. She is a loving mother to her son Luke and enjoys spending her free time with Yoga, walking in nature and reading. "Calming The Waters" is her first book.

Copyright©2022

Sylvia Schoderer Stevens

All Rights Reserved

Manufactured by Amazon.ca
Bolton, ON

29305673R00050